MW00769183

The Spanish Exploration of Florida

EXPLORATION AND DISCOVERY

EXPLORATION
AND DISCOVERY

The Spanish Exploration of Florida

The adventures of the Spanish conquistadors, including Juan Ponce de León, Pánfilo de Narváez, Alvar Núñez Cabeza de Vaca, Hernando de Soto, and Pedro Menéndez de Avilés, in the American south.

Bill and Dorcas Thompson

Mason Crest Publishers
Philadelphia

To Julian and Betty Alexander, Dottie Baird, and Martha Dismukes, along with countless other dear Florida friends, and especially to God, who through the writing of this book helped us to gain a love for the wonderful state of Florida in a way we had never known before.

Mason Crest Publishers
370 Reed Road
Broomall PA 19008

Mason Crest Publishers' world wide web address is
www.masoncrest.com

First printing

1 3 5 7 9 8 6 4 2

Library of Congress Cataloging-in-Publication Data on file at the Library of Congress

ISBN 1-59084-053-4

EXPLORATION AND DISCOVERY

Contents

SEPTEMTRIO

80   79

Cum Priuilegio.

Chiacha

Canara-gay

Coste

Guax-uli.

Xuala

Vllibahaly.

Xuaquile

Chalaqua

Quigata

Tafcalifa.

Cafaqui

Catilachegue

Rio de Canàas

Rio Iordan

Achusi

Aymay

Rio Sevo

al Spirito Santo

Culuta

Rio de Cañaueral

Rio de Flores

Rio de Nieues

P. de S. Maria.

Bayia baxa

Bayia de S. Iofeph.

S.Helena fliu.

P.S.Helena

ORIENS

Cruz

R. de los Mojes ui tuna

Baya de Baxos

Baya de Spo Santo

C. de Cruz.

C. Gruefo

Canal de Bahama

Iucayonoq3

Bahama

Iuan de Ponte

Rio de Corrento

C. de Cañareal

Aboa

Binini

LA FLORIDA.
Auctore Hieron. Chiaues.

Rio de Cañoas

Rio de pas

Rio de la florida

Martyres

Tortugas

Cancri

80   79

A Spanish Survivor

NO ONE WHO knew Alvar Núñez Cabeza de Vaca in Spain would have recognized him in Mexico. He was bone-thin, sickly looking, and half-naked, dressed in animal skins. Cabeza's feet were scarred and bloody after walking for 5,000 miles. His friends would also have been surprised at the people surrounding Cabeza. He was walking along a dusty path with a dozen Indians.

When this band of men heard the neighing of horses, they quickly stopped. Cabeza was filled with joy at the sound, but the Indians felt a surge of fear. The horses could only mean Spanish soldiers were in the area—a danger to natives. The Indians drew closer to Cabeza as if for protection. Suddenly, four Spanish soldiers came riding around a bend in the road.

The Spaniards spotted the group of natives and spurred their horses into a gallop. They had been hunting all day for such a sight. They needed slaves to work their silver mines, and most of the local Indians had scattered into the hills to escape. Now their long ride would have been worth it.

Just as the soldiers drew near to the group of men, Cabeza raised his hand and shouted out in Spanish. The soldiers brought their horses to a halt in surprise. Cabeza remembered, "They were dumfounded at the sight of me, strangely dressed and in company with Indians. They just stood staring for a long time."

No wonder they were shocked. It was the spring of 1536, and they were soldiers of conquistador Hernando Cortés. They were 1,000 miles from Mexico City and not far from the Pacific Ocean. The last thing they expected to see in that remote countryside was a dirty, ragged Spaniard in company with Indians!

Cabeza de Vaca was the first European to live among Indians on the North American continent. Yet he was not the first to seek fame and fortune in the land of Florida. This is the story, sometimes forgotten, of the influence Spain had on America during the century before the English Pilgrims landed at Jamestown or Plymouth Rock.

Alvar Núñez Cabeza de Vaca

Alvar Núñez Cabeza de Vaca was born around 1492 in Andalusia, a region of Spain near Cadiz. When his parents died, Cabeza went to live with an aunt and uncle. He became the *page* of a wealthy man while still a teenager and fought in Italy, where he was wounded in 1512. For 15 years, he fought for Spain against rebels and the French.

In 1528, Cabeza joined Pánfilo de Narváez's expedition to Florida. The expedition failed, and Cabeza was captured by natives in Texas in 1530. He escaped in 1534, and with three friends reached Spanish settlements in Mexico in 1536.

Cabeza returned to Spain in 1537, and in 1542 wrote *La Relacion,* a book about his trials in the New World. He was made governor of Paraguay in 1540 and tried to show kindness to the Indians because of what he had learned in Texas. His reforms were unpopular, however, and the colonists in Paraguay forced Cabeza to leave in 1544. In 1551, he was forbidden by the authorities in Spain to go back to the New World. He died in Spain around 1560.

The saga of Florida doesn't begin with the Spanish, however. Thousands of years before the Old World of Europe knew that there was a New World, Indians had settled in Florida and called it home. They had developed a culture all their own, far different from that of Europe.

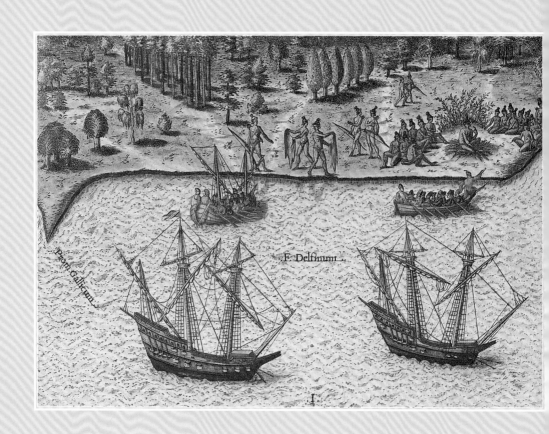

Prom. Gallicum

F. Delfinum

I

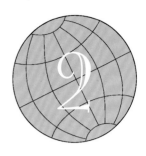

Spaniards landing in Florida are greeted by the native Americans who lived there in this 16th-century drawing. In reality, the native Floridians were fierce fighters, as numerous Spanish soldiers would discover.

Florida's First People

FLORIDA IS A land of water. Though it is over 400 miles long, the Atlantic Ocean and Gulf of Mexico are separated by only 120 miles. Lake Okeechobee is the second largest freshwater lake wholly within the United States. Florida is home to 30,000 other lakes, some as small as ponds, and it has over 1,700 streams and rivers. In the *brackish* marshes, where fresh water meets salt, fish and animal life abound.

It was on the coast, where oysters, crabs and fish were easy to catch, that native people first lived. They moved down from the north 12,000 years ago and found a home. As their population grew into an estimated 100,000 or more, they were scattered all over the peninsula. Some groups were related to each other through marriage and were close because of the same culture and language.

One of the largest of these groups was called the Timucua (tim'-uh-kwah). Timucua tribes stretched from Jacksonville on the east coast to Tampa Bay on the west coast. In the panhandle of Florida lived the Apalachee (ap-uh-latch'-ee), speaking their own language and following their own customs. The Calusa (ka-loo'-sah) tribes lived in the southwest, settling from Fort Myers on the coast to Lake Okeechobee. The Ais (ace) lived by the Indian River on the east coast, and the Tequesta (tee-kwest-uh) near present-day Miami.

Archaelogists, digging cautiously into the Florida soil, have uncovered the past. From ancient burial mounds, they have recovered pottery, ornaments and tools made and used by these native Americans. Dotted throughout Florida are shell **middens**, garbage dumps for these first Americans. From the shells and bones there, we learn what these people ate and how they lived.

When Europeans first arrived in Florida, they began to write down firsthand accounts of the Indians. Jacques Le Moyne, a Frenchmen who lived near the Timucua people in 1564, drew many pictures of them in their villages. Many Spaniards on expeditions to Florida sent detailed documents back to Europe. There are also letters and missionary

An example of a shell midden at the Timucan preserve on Talbot Island, near Jacksonville, Florida. By studying items found at these "garbage dumps," archaeologists have learned a lot about how the natives of Florida lived before the arrival of Spanish explorers during the 16th century.

reports that tell of personal experiences among the natives.

The villages were almost always located near water, either rivers, marshes or the ocean. A village had about 25 houses that were small and circular, set 75 feet apart from one another. The Indians built them out of palm leaves, wood and straw. Perhaps 200 people lived in one village.

The largest building was the communal meeting place where village elders met and public celebrations were held. Every village had a charnel house, where the bodies of the

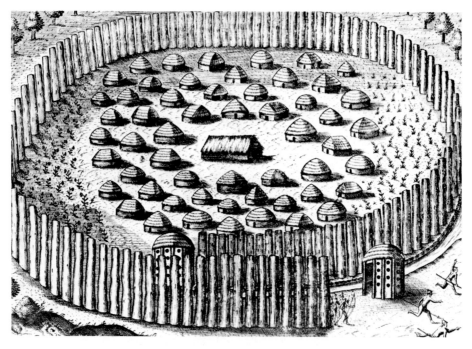

A drawing by the French artist Jacques Le Moyne shows a typical Florida Indian village. The large building in the center was a communal meeting place where village elders met and public celebrations were held. The bottom picture shows a modern-day version of a Timucua hut.

dead were placed until the skin fell from the bones. The bones were displayed to the people in another building that they might honor the dead. Then the bones were carefully placed in burial mounds.

The people were ruled by cacique, or chief, who was looked upon with great honor. The right to be a cacique was passed on from one generation to another through inheritance. Rulership went to the chief's nephew or niece through his oldest sister. Elders in the village would also receive their authority by inheritance and would be the chief's advisers. The rest of the people were commoners who usually remained in that position all their lives.

The natives of Florida were physically attractive people, over 6 feet tall with olive or brown colored skin. They were well-proportioned and good-looking to the Europeans who described them. They had great strength because of their way of life. Because they did not allow children with physical defects to live, there were no deformed adults.

The men had long black hair that they bound up around their heads. They braided it with dyed animal hair and decorated it with grass and feathers. In battles, they would use their topknot as a quiver for arrows. They wore only a deerskin loincloth, though in the north during winter, they put on leggings and moccasins of animal skins.

Indian women were strong and tall and wore their black hair down to their waists. Europeans saw them swim across a river holding a baby above water with one hand! Their only clothing was a skirt woven from Spanish moss that grew in the trees.

Both men and women tattooed their bodies in red, black and blue colors in beautiful designs. They painted their faces black or red with a blue fringe around their mouths. The decorated themselves with necklaces of shells and with bracelets and anklets of bone. In their pierced ears they placed pins of bone, shell or pearl. Some dangled flat plates of silver or brass from their legs that tinkled like bells as they walked.

Many tribes in the north began to develop agriculture early on in their history. The weather and soil allowed them to plant crops such as maize, pumpkins, and squash. This reliable food source made it possible for these people to have permanent settlements. The land was full of deer, raccoons, and rabbits for them to hunt. They also fished and gathered wild berries from the woods.

It was a different story in the south. The weather was too

This drawing by Theodore de Bry, a contemporary of Jacques Le Moyne, shows the Florida Indians cultivating their fields. The natives living in the north developed agriculture thousands of years before the Spaniards arrived.

hot and the soil too sandy for crops. Groups like the Calusa got their food from the water. The bays and rivers of southern Florida teem with life. Their 40-foot-high shell middens were filled with fish bones, crab claws, and oyster shells they took from the sea. To catch fish, they learned to make a gill net from hand-twisted palm fibers. Their nets had floats made from cypress trees with clam shells for weights.

The religion of the Florida Indians was similar all over the peninsula. They were close to the earth, so their worship was centered around the sun and sky as well as fire, earth's representative of the sun. The religious leader was called a shaman, who was the medicine man and handled religious ceremonies.

Many Florida Indians often fought each other and could be fierce in battle. Their main weapons were bows and arrows, wooden clubs, spears and stone hatchets. However, they even used their finger

A European named Fontaneda D'Escalante, who was held captive for 11 years by the Calusa, reported that these natives made human sacrifice in their worship. Fontaneda said the Calusa carried their victim to the top of a mound while singing and dancing. After cutting off his head, the eyes would be offered to their god. He wrote that sometimes captive Spanish sailors were sacrificed in this way.

nails. They sharpened them to a point and would cut an enemy's forehead in battle so the flowing blood would block their vision. They scalped those they killed and carried the hair on poles during celebrations.

They played games, including running and archery, but a certain ball game was their favorite. Several villages would compete to prove their superiority. They erected a tall goalpost with an eagle's nest on top containing a stuffed eagle. Two teams of 40 men would try to kick a small, hard buckskin ball at the post or at the nest. The struggles resembled warfare, and the result was often broken bones, the loss of sight, and even death. When the missionaries began to work among the Indians, they tried to abolish this ball game, but with little success.

The Florida natives were excellent artists. Indian pottery has been uncovered all over Florida. It is the oldest in the United States. The Calusa, especially, were experts in wood carving. Evidence of their skill has been unearthed on Marco Island in southwestern Florida. Much of their clothing was decorated with colorful designs and they painted large murals on their communal house walls.

As the 16th century dawned, the native way of life began to decline. Many died in battle, because the natives could not match the technology of the Europeans with their advanced weapons. They were also often outnumbered.

Because the Calusa depended so much upon water, they became expert sailors. To build their large canoes, they set fire to the inside of

cypress tress and then carved out the center. They were strong and powerful people and may have paddled all the way to Cuba for trading purposes. This drawing was made by Jacques Le Moyne.

Slavery, imposed by the sword, drained them of health and purpose. One 16th-century Spaniard wrote that the Indians were exhausted by the work demanded of them. They had "affliction and fatigue of their spirits because they had lost the liberty God had given them; for the Spanish treated them worse than slaves."

Their most deadly enemy, however, was disease. They did not have the *immunity* to fight off illnesses brought by explorers from Europe. Smallpox, measles, typhoid fever, and others began to kill off the Native Americans almost immediately. *Epidemics* were already being reported by Columbus only a few years after he landed in 1492.

An idealized painting of Ponce de León and his men drinking the water of Florida, hoping to find the Fountain of Youth. No one knows for sure whether Ponce really believed the legends about the fountain. His main purpose for exploring Florida was to find gold and glory as a conquistador.

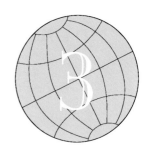

The Adventures of Ponce de León

JUAN PONCE DE León stood at the harbor of Cadíz in Spain on a spring day in 1493. It was from this port that many ships would sail to the New World. Ponce de León had gone to Cadíz to visit some relatives and see the ships Christopher Columbus was preparing for a voyage across the Atlantic.

Ponce de León was part of great changes taking place in Europe at the end of the 15th century. He was a veteran of the war against the Moors, who had first invaded Spain in 711. After nearly 800 years, the last Moorish stronghold had been taken in 1492. Now, like other soldiers and knights in Spain, he was looking for new opportunities.

Isabella and Ferdinand, rulers of Spain, had supported Columbus in his first voyage across the Atlantic in 1492. Believing the world to be smaller than it is, Columbus had expected to find a route to India and China by going west across the Atlantic. The spices and silk that came from those countries were worth their weight in gold when brought back to sell in Europe.

Columbus had returned on March 14, 1493, and brought news of a New World. He was eager for a second voyage. A letter he had written to one of his sponsors was published in April of 1493, and his discovery of new lands

In the 15th century, the modern country of Spain was made up of several smaller kingdoms. When King Ferdinand and Queen Isabella married, they united their kingdoms, Aragon and Castille, into a powerful country.

was being talked about all over Europe. That same year, the Catholic Pope, Alexander VI, gave Spain the right to settle the New World and convert its people to Christianity.

Juan Ponce de León was able to get a place on this second voyage as one of the 1,200 or more people crammed on the vessels. Along with the passengers were the first horses and pigs that would come to the New World. Ponce de León even took cats to kill any mice that might turn up in the *granaries*. After the ships were fitted and supplies were stored, the fleet left Cadíz on September 25, 1493.

In a month, the fleet reached the island of Hispaniola, today known as the Dominican Republic and Haiti. The colony Columbus had left there was burned to the ground and the settlers murdered by local Indians. Columbus began immediately to build another town.

Over the next few years, Juan Ponce de León helped to subdue the Indians. As a reward, he was given land on Espanola and made adelantado, or governor, of the eastern part of the island. He was later named ***adelantado*** of the nearby unexplored island of Puerto Rico and built a colony there in August 1509. Ponce de León tried to be fair with the peaceful Indians and spoke up against their mistreatment.

Ponce de León became interested in talk he heard among the natives about an unexplored island to the north called Bimini. The Indians believed that there was a Fountain of Youth there that could keep a person young. Such a legend had been talked about in Europe for years.

Though Ponce de León may have included a search for the Fountain of Youth in his journeys, his real desire was for new land to settle, as well as discovering the long-sought passage to India. Europeans still believed that Florida was an island off the coast of Asia. Ponce de León went to Spain for permission to look for the land of Bimini. On February 23, 1512, he signed a contract with King Ferdinand to settle and govern Bimini.

Juan Ponce de León returned to his farm on Hispaniola and equipped three ships with about 65 people for the adventure ahead. They sailed on March 4, 1513, and headed north. The party sighted land for the first time on Easter Day. Ponce de León landed a week later on April 3, 1513. He claimed the land for the king of Spain and called it "Pascua Florida." Florida had its name—Feast of Flowers—named after Easter, the season of flowers.

Ponce de León sailed south along the coast of Florida and landed again somewhere south of Fort Pierce. He had his first encounter with the Florida natives there, probably the Ais. A group of natives approached the Spaniards and began to take their supplies. When one of Ponce de León's sailors was knocked unconscious, a fight broke out. Two of

Juan Ponce de León

Juan Ponce de León was born in the northern province of Valladolid in Spain, sometime between 1560 and 1574. Little is known of his early life, but he fought against the Moors in Granada in 1492 and learned warfare and leadership. He sailed with Columbus on his second voyage to the New World in 1493.

Ponce de León led campaigns against the Indians on Hispaniola between 1502 and 1504 and helped settle the island of Puerto Rico in 1509. In 1511, he imported the first native Africans into Puerto Rico as slave labor.

Ponce de León was appointed governor of Puerto Rico by King Ferdinand of Spain, but was replaced in 1512. The next year, he explored the east coast of a new land which he called "Pascua Florida." While returning to Puerto Rico, he landed on the Yúcatan Peninsula of Mexico. Ponce also discovered the Bahama Channel, which allowed Spanish ships to sail from the Caribbean into the Atlantic.

From 1515 to 1521, Ponce fought against the Carib Indians on the islands of the Caribbean. In 1521, he returned to Florida. Wounded by the Calusa Indians on the west coast of Florida, he was taken to Cuba, where he died in July 1521.

his men were wounded, and one native was taken captive. Ponce de León had hoped to develop peaceful relations with the Indians and was surprised at their hostility.

Because of this unexpected and unexplained behavior, it is believed that Ponce de León was not the first Spaniard to land in Florida. After the Spanish had settled Hispaniola, disease and mistreatment began killing off the natives. To find laborers, Spaniards may have made slave-raids on the Florida peninsula. As a result of these earlier, unrecorded voyages, the Indians of Florida had become wary of these white "invaders."

Ponce de León sailed south through the Florida Keys and then north to the vicinity of Port Charlotte on Florida's west coast. When they anchored there for water and fire-wood, the Calusa Indians came to see what they were doing and tried to grab their anchor cables. Twenty canoes attacked the ships. Some Calusas were killed and others captured. As Ponce de León explored the west coast, there were further conflicts with the natives. Ponce de León decided to head back to Hispaniola and return later.

Ponce de León went back to Spain in April 1514 to report his discovery of Florida. When he arrived, he was knighted by Ferdinand and given a personal coat of arms, the first conquistador ever to receive one. He was now "Don" (sir) Juan Ponce de León.

was being talked about all over Europe. That same year, the Catholic Pope, Alexander VI, gave Spain the right to settle the New World and convert its people to Christianity.

Juan Ponce de León was able to get a place on this second voyage as one of the 1,200 or more people crammed on the vessels. Along with the passengers were the first horses and pigs that would come to the New World. Ponce de León even took cats to kill any mice that might turn up in the *granaries*. After the ships were fitted and supplies were stored, the fleet left Cadíz on September 25, 1493.

In a month, the fleet reached the island of Hispaniola, today known as the Dominican Republic and Haiti. The colony Columbus had left there was burned to the ground and the settlers murdered by local Indians. Columbus began immediately to build another town.

Over the next few years, Juan Ponce de León helped to subdue the Indians. As a reward, he was given land on Hispanola and made *adelantado*, or governor, of the eastern part of the island. He was later named adelantado of the nearby unexplored island of Puerto Rico and built a colony there in August 1509. Ponce de León tried to be fair with the peaceful Indians and spoke up against their mistreatment.

Ponce de León became interested in talk he heard among the natives about an unexplored island to the north

Ponce de León's men carry the body of their wounded leader back to their ship. The arrow that hit Ponce in the thigh may have been poisoned. The Spanish explorer would not recover from the wound.

Somewhere around July 1, 1521, the group had difficulty with the Calusa again. It was a disaster for the Spaniards. They were unprepared for the fighting ability of the Calusa and were driven off of Florida. Juan Ponce de León was seriously wounded by a Calusa arrow. It entered his thighbone and could not be removed. It quickly became infected, and

Ponce de León came down with a high fever.

The ships sailed to Cuba, where they hoped their leader would recover. However, Don

Ponce de León's remains are in a marble tomb in San Juan Cathedral on Puerto Rico.

Juan Ponce de León died shortly after his return. When he was buried later in Puerto Rico, these words were carved on his tomb: "Here rest the bones of a valiant Lion (León), mightier in deeds than in name."

Though Ponce de León failed in Spain's first attempt to settle Florida, he is remembered as an honest man who treated the Indians with fairness. He was also the first to discover the Gulf Stream off the east coast of Florida on his first journey in 1513 and the first to explore the coast of Mexico and the Gulf Coast.

It would be seven years before another Spaniard would organize a second fleet and try to succeed where Juan Ponce de León had failed. However, that was to be an even greater failure—and at a much greater cost of life.

Alvar Núñez Cabeza de Vaca looks out over
the American southwest. Cabeza de Vaca
was a member of Pánfilo de Narváez's
failed expedition to Florida; he spent years
wandering through the region before finally
reaching the safety of Spanish settlements
in Mexico in 1536.

The Doomed Expedition of Narváez

ALVAR NÚÑEZ CABEZA DE VACA stood at the rail of a ship sailing for Florida. The king had appointed him treasurer of a new expedition. All of the explorations of the New World were private ventures, funded by the individuals who led them, but approved by the crown. As the king's representative, Cabeza would make sure the king received his share of the profits.

The head of the forces that landed that April day in 1528 was Pánfilo de Narváez. Narváez had provided the money for the expedition. In return, he was given power over the territory and the right to much of its wealth. Narváez hoped to find the kind of treasure that Hernán

Cortés had discovered in Mexico only a few years before. Narváez had a reputation for being cruel and stupid. He was even called incompetent by some who knew him. That reputation was about to be proven true.

Narváez reached the coast of Florida with 400 men and anchored off Tampa Bay. He walked across the sand and claimed the land for the king of Spain. After two days, Narváez and de Vaca went inland with 40 soldiers to investigate the land and search for food. They passed through several small native villages, but found little to eat. When they discovered a small amount of gold at one village, they became excited at the prospect of finding wealth. The natives told them that there was much gold and food to be found if they continued to travel north along the coast to a land they called Apalachee.

When the men returned to their ships, Narváez decided to take 300 men and venture inland while the ships sailed north along the coast with the rest of the crew. They were to look for a harbor and meet up with the inland group. Cabeza de Vaca disagreed, believing that the party should stay together. They had little food, were not in shape to travel, and were not sure of where to meet. In spite of Cabeza's concerns, however, the majority decided to travel inland. Cabeza, reluctant to appear cowardly, went with Narváez as their ships sailed away.

Pánfilo de Narváez

Narváez was born around 1478 in Valladolid, Spain. As a young man, he entered military service. He went to the New World and was one of the first to settle the island of Jamaica. He served with Diego Velasquez and helped conquer Cuba, where he lived for a while. In 1520, he was sent to Mexico by Velasquez, the governor of Cuba, to capture and replace Hernán Cortés. He lost an eye in battle, was defeated, and put in prison by Cortés in Mexico. Narváez returned to Cuba, and in 1526 was given a contract by Charles V to settle Florida. Arriving in Tampa Bay in May 1528 and marching north, Narváez reached the panhandle of Florida by July. Narváez's army built boats to sail to Mexico. Sometime in November 1528, Narváez presumably drowned when his boat was swept out to sea.

On May 1, the land party traveled north. For two weeks they could find no Indian village or any food supply. With their food *rations* from the ship almost gone and the men faint from hunger, they fortunately found a village with enough food for them all. They captured some villagers to act as guides and continued heading north. By the middle of June, they reached the area of the Apalachee.

After a month in the area, the Narváez party found no trace of gold and few villages or farms where they could get supplies. They decided to move toward the coast, where they had been told they would find more food. As they crossed a deep lake, they were suddenly attacked by Indians hidden in the trees that surrounded them.

They fought off this Indian attack and arrived at a deserted village near the coast. The natives, warned of the Spaniards' approach, had taken their village food supply and left. By this time, some of the soldiers had died, others were wounded, and many were sick from lack of food and rest. Soon, a third of the men were ill. They moved on, trying to reach open water.

Once at the coast, they decided to build boats and sail toward the Spanish settlements in Mexico. No one in the party had any idea how far they would have to go, since no European had yet explored the territory they were in.

They made nails, saws, axes, and other tools out of their stirrups, spurs, and crossbows. For food, they killed a horse every third day. The men made pitch from pine trees, and cords and rigging from the tails and manes of their horses. They used their shirts for sails and made oars from the juniper trees near them. Finally, they crafted water bottles from horsehide they had tanned.

On September 22, a month and a half after they had begun to build, they were ready to leave. By this time, 40 men had died from sickness, from earlier wounds, and from frequent attacks by the Indians. They sailed away in five vessels with 50 men in each, so crowded that they could barely move.

After a month, while passing the Mississippi River, a strong current and heavy north wind blew them out to sea, where two of the boats were lost. Later, the boat carrying Narváez was also swept out to sea. Another storm separated the two remaining boats, but Cabeza de Vaca's managed to reach an island just off the modern state of Texas. They met some peaceful Indians who fed them, but when the men tried to leave the island, their boat *capsized*, and three were drowned.

As the naked survivors huddled among the dunes, cold from the November wind, Indians from the island approached them. Cabeza remembered: "We were in such a plight that one could have counted our bones without difficulty. We looked like the image of death." Then the natives did a surprising thing, said Cabeza: "When the Indians saw the disaster that had come upon us . . . with so much ill luck and misery, they sat down among us and, with the great grief and pity they felt on seeing us in such a desperate plight, all of them began to weep loudly."

Not much later, men from the other boat reached the same area and rejoined their friends with joy. They all decided to winter on the island. During those bitter months, 75 of the 90 men who had made it there died.

In the spring of 1529, the Spaniards separated. Thirteen of them headed for Mexico, never to be heard of again. One remained on the island, and Cabeza de Vaca, too sick to travel, was taken by natives to the mainland. It was the beginning of four years of hardship. Many times during those years, he was nothing more than a slave. He remembered: "I had to gather the roots they used for food, under water and among the reeds; my fingers were so lacerated from this that if a blade of straw touched them they bled."

Things improved, however, as Cabeza began to trade goods among the tribes of that area. Since he was an outsider, he could more easily exchange items between tribes who were normally hostile to each other. One day, while trading, some Indians told him about other men who looked like him. Soon de Vaca was reunited with these other Spanish castaways who had lived among a different tribe.

The Native Americans regarded Cabeza and his friends as different. One day, they were asked to breathe over a sick Indian with the hope of curing him. Cabeza and his friends prayed the rosary, the Lord's Prayer, and whatever else came to mind. The man reported that he felt better. Cabeza and the others gained reputations as healers and medicine men.

The four men planned to escape the life they were living as slaves. Until they found the right opportunity, however, they knew they had to stay alive as best they could. In September 1534, while the Indians were celebrating a festival, the four finally slipped away and began traveling west. They continued their journey into the spring of 1535 and crossed the Rio Grande, a river unknown to them. Without knowing it, they were entering Mexico.

After so much trouble in the past with coastal Indians, they were surprised by the warm welcome received by the inland tribes. Later, they entered a more prosperous area in northwestern Mexico, not far from the Pacific Ocean. It was during this time that they saw signs of their countrymen. Their long, painful exile finally ended in 1536 when they encountered Spanish soldiers.

The four survivors traveled another 1,000 miles before they reached Mexico City. Once there, they were greeted with honor. Cabeza was so accustomed to his rough life, that at first he could barely wear clothes and needed to sleep on the ground.

Cabeza reached Spain in 1537 and wrote about his amazing survival. His memoirs, titled *Relacion*, inspired others to explore this New World and seek the wealth that they felt Cabeza had missed. Some were convinced that just over the horizon waited golden cities for them to plunder.

No one is certain where Hernando de Soto landed when he arrived in Florida in May of 1539. A memorial to de Soto was erected near this beach on the southern side of Tampa Bay.

De Soto and his Inland Journey

HERNANDO DE SOTO watched Cabeza de Vaca at the Spanish court as Cabeza spoke with King Charles. Cabeza was excited about what he had learned in his years among the Indians. He had hoped to receive a contract from the king to return to Florida as the leader of his own expedition. However, de Soto had already been given that permission and was ready to sail.

De Soto had dreamed of traveling to the New World since he was a child. At age 14, he became *page* to a wealthy man in Seville. He sailed with him to the New World in 1514. At age 17, de Soto went with Francisco Pizarro to Peru and helped him conquer the Inca Empire.

He went back to Europe a wealthy man at the age of 38.

Once back in Spain, De Soto was ready to be leader of his own expedition. He hoped to convince Cabeza to go with him so he could use what Cabeza had learned about the uncharted territory of Florida. However, Cabeza de Vaca would not accept his offer. Cabeza wanted to lead an expedition of his own and received the governorship of Paraguay. He also must have known of De Soto's reputation for his harsh treatment of Indians in Peru.

Hernando de Soto had no trouble finding other men to join him, however. His success in Peru and the vast wealth he had earned made others want to travel with him. Using half of his money, de Soto equipped a new fleet of nine ships and over 600 men. In April 1538, his fleet sailed for Cuba

Hernando de Soto had helped another conquistador, Francisco Pizarro, conquer the wealthy Inca empire in Peru. With fewer than 200 soldiers, Pizarro and de Soto captured the Inca ruler, Atahalpula, and took control of the region. The treasures of the Incas—gold, silver, and jewels—were sent back to Spain, making it a wealthy nation and de Soto a rich man. De Soto used the money he had earned from the conquest of Peru to pay for his expedition into Florida.

with trumpets blaring and cannons roaring.

On May 18, 1539, after repairs in Cuba, de Soto sailed north to Florida. His ships arrived at Tampa Bay on May 30 with 213 horses, 600 men, and two women. He was well equipped with supplies and had a large herd of pigs for food. Once again, Florida was claimed for the king of Spain. De Soto looked with confidence on his army, satisfied that he would succeed where Narváez had not.

Soon the army encountered hostile Indians. These *aborigines* had not forgotten the cruelty of earlier Spaniards arriving on their shores. However, the Spaniards felt well prepared. They were convinced their weapons were far superior to those of the Indians. The Spaniards used crossbows, which could shoot a short arrow with great power and *halberds*, long lances with an axe head. Their swords were of steel, and they wore chain mail all over their bodies. They carried shields for added protection. The foot soldiers were armed with 12-foot *pikes* and the *arquebus*, a matchlock musket. The officers had horses trained to charge in battle and trample any opposition. In addition, de Soto arrived with a pack of large dogs—mastiffs, greyhounds, and wolfhounds—that could tear an enemy apart. He would not hesitate to use them whenever necessary.

Hernando de Soto soon discovered that fighting Florida natives was not the same as fighting the Indians of Peru.

The arquebus had a pan filled with powder on top of the long wooden shaft. A small metal holder in front of the pan held the match—a hemp rope—that would be left to smolder. The soldier pulled a lever that brought the hemp match down into the pan. The powder would ignite, and the flame would set off the main barrel charge.

There, the natives had offered little resistance and controlling them was not difficult. They were not a warlike people. It was a different matter in Florida. In fighting the Timucua, one of the Spaniards said: "They are never quiet but always running and crossing from side to side so that crossbows . . . cannot be aimed at them; and before a crossbowman can fire a shot, an Indian can shoot 3 or 4 arrows, and very seldom does he miss what he shoots at."

The army discovered that the Indians' accuracy and swiftness was not their only problem. Arrows aimed at their chain mail would split into pieces and pass through into a soldier's body, creating wounds that became infected. Also, the humid, rainy weather of Florida quickly rusted the iron mail. Furthermore, their muskets were inaccurate and took a long time to ignite. When wet, they wouldn't work at all. The weapons and armor soon became a burden as they traveled through the intense heat. Their superior equipment did not give them the advantage they expected.

Early in de Soto's journey, seeing Indians in a field, he began to attack. A naked, sunburned white man, tattooed like the natives, stepped out of the group. He called out, "Sirs, I am a Christian; do not kill me. Do not kill these Indians for they have given me my life." The man was Juan Ortiz. He had been with Narváez, but was captured by Indians and had been with them for 12 years. Ortiz joined de Soto's expedition and served for the next three years as interpreter.

The Spanish army moved inland and up the coast looking for gold as others had in Mexico and Peru. When they came to an Indian village, de Soto would take the chief hostage to make sure the Indians would cause him no trou-

Juan Ortiz had been a member of Pánfilo de Narváez's doomed expedition to Florida 11 years earlier. He had been captured by native Floridians and tortured before escaping. He found shelter with another tribe. When he saw the tall masts of Hernando de Soto's ships, he and three Indians came to investigate. De Soto soon asked Ortiz to join his party as an interpreter.

Hernando de Soto

De Soto was born in southwestern Spain around 1496. He was from a noble family but a poor one. He sought his future as a soldier and sailed to Central America in 1513 with Pedro Arias Davila, the new governor of Panama. In 1524, de Soto helped in the conquest of Nicaragua, where he stayed and helped rule the region. In 1531, he joined Francisco Pizarro in conquering Peru. De Soto returned to Spain in 1536 a wealthy man.

On April 20, 1536, de Soto was made governor and captain-general of Cuba and Florida by King Charles V of Spain. In May 1539, he sailed for Florida with over 600 soldiers. De Soto landed at Tampa Bay on May 30 and set out in search of the kind of wealth he had found in Peru. The army spent their first winter in northern Florida and in early 1540 traveled north into Georgia. For the next two years, de Soto sought in vain for gold in South and North Carolina, Tennessee, Alabama, Mississippi, Arkansas, Louisiana, and Texas. He discovered the Mississippi River on May 8, 1541.

Sick, discouraged, and defeated, de Soto died on May 21, 1542. He was buried in the Mississippi River.

ble. When the army moved on, de Soto would make the chief give him Indian helpers, who would be chained together as a human baggage train. Then, those captives were released when they were replaced by new slaves taken from the next tribe the army met.

In late October 1539, the army reached Apalachee in the panhandle of Florida. Their search for gold wasn't successful, but they found large quantities of food and decided to winter there. De Soto discovered they were only 25 miles from the Gulf of Mexico and sent troops to investigate. These men found horse skulls left by Narváez's men when building their boats nine years before.

De Soto sent troops back to Tampa Bay with an order for his ships to sail north. The fleet arrived at the end of December and anchored in what is now Pensacola Bay. De Soto took supplies from the ships and sent them back to Cuba for more provisions. They were to return to Pensacola Bay that next summer. They were told, if the army was not there, to return the following summer.

It was a difficult winter for the Spaniards and their captive Indians. They fortified the Indian village they were using, but were constantly attacked by angry natives who resisted their presence in Apalachee. Twice during the winter months, the village was set on fire and they lost some supplies. During the severe weather, most of the Indian slaves died from hunger or exposure to the cold. Morale among the army began to decline from hunger and boredom.

On March 3, 1540, as the winter ended, the Spanish army left Apalachee and traveled north into Georgia. Due to the loss of their Indian slaves, the soldiers had to carry their own supplies, either on their backs or on their horses. At times, the woods were so thick, they could not search for the Indians who attacked them from the trees. This kind of **guerrilla** warfare was difficult for de Soto to handle, and it continued throughout his journey.

For the next two years, de Soto traveled through 10 of today's southern states. At one point, in present-day Georgia, his troops wanted to stop and build a settlement in the fertile countryside. It wasn't far from the Atlantic Ocean, and they believed they could farm and develop trade. De Soto was determined to press on, however, hearing of a land to the west where there might be gold.

Moving through the Carolinas, de Soto crossed the Appalachian Mountains into Tennessee and then into Alabama. In July 1540, his forces had a difficult setback when Indian forces burned a village where de Soto's army had camped. They lost many of their supplies, weapons, horses, and even clothes. By this time, 100 Spaniards had died since landing at Tampa Bay.

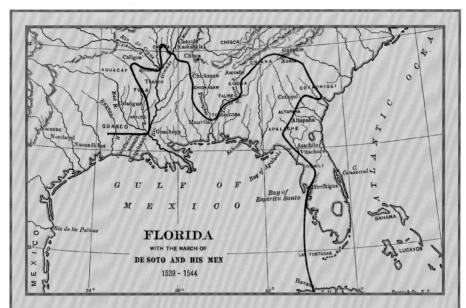

This map of Florida and the southern region of what today is the United States shows the winding route Hernando de Soto and his men followed during their long exploration of the region.

In the spring of 1541, de Soto's army was again attacked by a strong force of Indians and suffered great losses. A dozen of his men were killed, many were wounded, 50 horses were destroyed, and most of his pigs were burned in a fire. The 450 remaining men were discouraged, half naked, and exhausted. Their bitterness turned into criticism of de Soto's leadership.

The weary army wandered on, seemingly without any definite purpose. De Soto even began to consider the possibility of giving up. On May 3, 1541, they reached a powerful river, now called the Mississippi. Though it had been seen by Narváez's men in 1528, de Soto has been given credit for first sighting it.

Crossing the Mississippi, the army moved through Arkansas and camped there for the winter. Hearing of a "great water" from the Indians, de Soto decided to find this water in the spring, build boats, and send men to Cuba for supplies and reinforcements

Juan Ortiz died during that winter. Without him, it was almost impossible to communicate with the natives. In the spring, de Soto sent men to look for the sea, but they could find no trace of it. De Soto became deeply depressed. He had been sick for some time with a fever and now became seriously ill. He put one of his officers in charge and made his will. Then, on May 21, 1542, he died. His body was secretly buried in the Mississippi River so the natives would

In an eerie midnight ceremony, Hernando de Soto's body is dropped into the Mississippi River. The Spaniards had tried to make the Native Americans believe that their leader was a god, so they secretly buried de Soto in the river and told the natives that he had returned to heaven.

not discover his death.

His army then traveled west with the hope of reaching Mexico. They traveled for months, but the land became more and more barren. They reached the modern state of Texas with no idea of how far away Mexico was. They decided to return to the Mississippi River.

At the river, they built a *forge*, cut down timber, and with the help of a shipbuilder and carpenters among them, built seven ships. They finished in June 1543 and began their journey toward the sea. In spite of severe Indian attacks along the river, they reached the Gulf of Mexico in 17 days. After some rest and repairing of their battered boats, they sailed into the Gulf of Mexico.

Hugging the coast for fear of the open sea, they sailed for two months. Finally, on September 10, the weary army saw a settlement along a wide river. Near exhaustion, they asked where they were. They received an answer in Spanish! They had reached Panuco, a settlement of New Spain.

With the failures of Ponce de León, Narváez, and now Hernando de Soto, was it all a tragic waste? They had all hoped to establish a Spanish stronghold in Florida, gain wealth for themselves and Christianize the natives. None of them had reached their goals. Spanish authorities soon became disinterested in exploring Florida further.

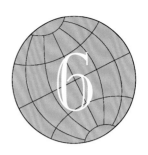

St Augustine: A Spanish Success Story

ON SEPTEMBER 8, 1565, Seloy, a Timucua Indian chief, stood watching the Spanish fleet anchor offshore. From his great house, he watched as Pedro Menéndez de Avilés stepped ashore from a small boat and knelt. The bright sun glistened off a silver cross mounted on a long wooden pole above the head of Menéndez. Chief Seloy welcomed these strangers to his village and offered them shelter in his own home. Before the week was out, Menéndez had his men dig a moat around the chief's house and begin erecting a *palisade* of logs around the area. Menéndez converted the area into a fort and named it St. Augustine, because for Catholics it was the day to honor this particular saint.

Pedro Menéndez de Avilés

Pedro Menéndez de Avilés, one of 21 brothers and sisters, was born on February 15, 1519, in Avilés, Spain. He became a seaman when a young man and fought with French ships off the coast of western Europe. Later, he became a commander of Spanish treasure ships sailing between Mexico and Spain.

In the early 1560s, King Philip II sent Menéndez to Florida to rid that area of the French. He assembled a fleet and sailed for Florida, reaching it in September 1565. After wiping out French troops, he began a plan to develop the Florida colony. Poor food supplies, conflict with the Indians, and mutinies among the settlers, however, undermined his hopes.

Menéndez was eventually made governor of Cuba and spent some time there. The king called him back to Spain to prepare an *armada* against the English. In the middle of his preparations, Pedro Menéndez de Avilés died on September 17, 1574.

It was the Spanish king, Philip II, who had sent these ships to the New World. Europe had changed in the 52 years since Ponce de León had first sighted the land he called Florida. Other European powers were now disputing

Spain's right to the American continent. They argued that the Pope had no authority to assign the New World to Spain as he had done in 1493.

News had reached Philip that France was attempting to plant a colony somewhere along the eastern coast of Florida. Philip knew that he needed to build a settlement to justify his claim to this land. He was also deeply concerned about protecting his treasure ships sailing from Mexico. As Spanish vessels loaded with gold and silver sailed up the east coast of Florida bound for Spain, they were being robbed by French pirates. Ships wrecked by storms were being plundered on both coasts by the Calusa and the Ais. The survivors were either killed or enslaved. Spain needed a settlement that would provide protection and refuge.

When King Philip learned that the French had already built Fort Caroline on the east coast of Florida, he ordered Menéndez to get rid of the French forces. "We hold it to be a very important thing to defeat these Frenchmen and expel them from the province of Florida," Philip said.

Menéndez sailed for Cadíz with 1,000 people, including 300 soldiers sent by the king. Before he left, he learned that reinforcements were being sent to Fort Caroline. Menéndez hurried to reach Florida before the French ships did.

However, he was too late. The French fleet was already docked at Fort Caroline, so Menéndez went 40 miles south and landed at the Indian village of Seloy, renaming the area St. Augustine. There he began building a fort of his own. French ships, sent to attack St. Augustine, were wrecked by a storm. Realizing that Fort Caroline was undermanned, he gathered 500 men and headed overland to attack it.

The Spanish army traveled four days through the marshy land in pouring rain. Wet and tired, they attacked the fort at dawn. The French were unprepared and taken completely by surprise. The frightened French soldiers were soon overpowered. Some escaped over the wall, but most were killed. Menéndez spared only the women, children, and a few men who could be useful to him. The French threat to Spanish control of Florida was over.

Pedro Menéndez was now ready to begin his ambitious plan to turn Florida into a profitable province of Spain. He wanted to develop colonies which could develop trade with Spain, have missionaries convert the natives to the Catholic faith, and build a military base for Spain.

His first step was to win the friendship of the Indians and bring peace to the peninsula. At the same time, he began to

Solis de Meras, brother-in-law of Menéndez, accompanied him on his trip to St. Augustine. His journals, translated in 1964, have become one of the most important sources of information about Menéndez and St. Augustine.

The French flag flies over this reconstruction of Fort Caroline, the settlement built by the French in Florida during the early 1560s. Menéndez and his men destroyed the French fort in 1565.

build forts around the peninsula to protect to settlers and missionaries and to control the natives. In 1566, Menéndez sailed through the Florida Keys and into the region of the Calusa. Once there, he and his men entered the town of a powerful chief, Carlos.

The Spanish forces marched in to the sound of *fifes*, drums, and trumpets, hoping to impress the chief. Carlos seemed unmoved. After talking, trading, and expressing friendship, Menéndez and Carlos signed a peace treaty, the first of its kind in Florida. To seal the agreement, Menéndez agreed to marry Carlos' sister. His main reason for doing this probably was to develop strong ties with this fierce tribe.

The following year, Menéndez built a fort near Carlos's village. Among the men stationed there was a Jesuit priest sent to teach the Catholic faith to the natives. Menéndez built another fort in the Tampa Bay area among the Timucua people and one in Tequesta territory, near modern-day Miami. In each area, Menéndez planned to bring development, protection to settlers, and Christianity.

However, his plan for Florida was unsuccessful. Menéndez was named governor of Cuba and was often gone from Florida. The soldiers were unable to keep peace with the Indians and had several conflicts with them. Farms were difficult to protect and were often raided by the Indians.

Menéndez returned to Spain to help the king in another matter and died shortly thereafter in 1574. Only two years after his death, the forts he had built were either

The Spanish coat of arms is carved into a wall at Castillo San Marcos, a Spanish fort in St. Augustine, Florida. Unlike European settlers in the north, many of the Spaniards in St. Augustine married native women, and the two cultures began to integrate. Their children were called mestizos. It is this blend of cultures that sets Spanish settlement in the New World apart from that of other nations.

destroyed or abandoned. Only St. Augustine remained. It became the only Spanish settlement in Florida.

The settlers struggled to survive. The town was attacked often by both Indians and other European powers. Several times, St. Augustine was almost burned to the ground. It had frequent storms and disease. Hunger was often a problem with farms hard to protect and supplies slow to arrive. Yet in spite of these difficulties, St. Augustine survived and today is the oldest permanent European settlement in North America.

Today, archaeologists at St. Augustine are bringing the past to life. Nearly 1,400 *potsherds* have been found. They have uncovered glass beads used for trading with the Indians. Copper straight pins, carved wood, and small lead shot balls, used for hunting, give us more evidence of everyday life in Menéndez's day. Connections with Spain remain, too. Every year in February, a weekend is set aside to celebrate the birthday of Pedro Menéndez de Avilés.

Spain had a powerful and lasting effect on Florida in the 16th century. From Juan Ponce de León to Pedro Menéndez de Avilés, Spanish influence spread across the peninsula. We must never forget that part of our heritage as a nation is Hispanic. St. Augustine, with its Spanish architecture and Spanish celebrations, will always be a reminder for us.

Chronology

1492 Columbus makes his first voyage to the New World.

1493 Juan Ponce de León arrives in Hispaniola on Columbus' second voyage.

1512 Ponce de León receives permission from King Ferdinand to settle the island of Bimini.

1513 Ponce de León lands on the east coast of the peninsula and names it "Pascua Florida."

1514 Ponce de León receives an appointment to settle and govern Florida.

1521 Ponce de León makes a second voyage to Florida, is wounded, and dies in Cuba.

1528 Pánfilo de Narváez and Cabeza de Vaca land in Florida.

1528 Narváez dies, and Cabeza de Vaca lives among native Americans for the next seven years.

1539 Hernando de Soto lands with 600 men at Tampa Bay.

1542 De Soto dies and is buried in the Mississippi River.

1543 Survivors of the de Soto expedition arrive in Mexico.

1565 Pedro Menéndez de Avilés founds St. Augustine, the oldest permanent European settlement on the North American continent.

1574 Menéndez dies in Europe.

1576 Spanish forts in Florida are destroyed or abandoned. St. Augustine alone survives.

Glossary

Aborigine—a person who is native to the area and descendant of the earliest known inhabitants of an area.

Adelantado—a Spanish governor in the New World.

Archaeologist—a scientist who searches for and studies remains of life from the past.

Armada—a fleet of warships.

Arquebus—a heavy matchlock gun used in the 15th and 16th centuries; developed in Europe.

Brackish—salty and unappealing to taste.

Capsize—to become upset or overturned, usually into water.

Epidemic—affecting a large number of people within a population or region at the same time.

Fife—a small flute.

Forge—a shop where metal is heated and worked into shapes.

Granary—container or bin to hold grains.

Guerrilla—warfare which is not open combat; usually surprise attacks from a hiding position.

Halberd—a long-handled knife-like weapon, with the end shaped like an axe.

Immunity—the body's power to resist disease.

Glossary

Middens—a garbage heap.

Page—a young boy who serves as an attendant to a person of rank.

Palisade—a fence made of wooden stakes around a town to defend against attackers.

Pike—a heavy spear with a very long shaft.

Potsherds—pieces or fragments of broken pottery vessels found by archaeologists in their excavations.

Ration—a food allowance for one day.

Further Reading

Brown, Robin. *Florida's First People: 12,000 Years of Human History.*
Sarasota, Fl. Pineapple Press, 1994.

Fuson, Robert A. *Juan Ponce de León and the Spanish Discovery of Puerto Rico and Florida.* Blacksburg, Va.: McDonald and Woodward Publishing, 2000.

Gallagher, Jim. *Hernando de Soto and the Exploration of Florida.* Philadelphia: Chelsea House, 2000.

Howard, David A. *Conquistador in Chains: Cabeza de Vaca and the Indians of North America.* Tuscaloosa: University of Alabama Press, 1997.

Manucy, Albert. *Sixteenth Century St. Augustine: The People and Their Houses.* Gainesville: University of Florida Press, 1997.

Internet Resources

Juan Ponce de León

http://www.stamponhistory.com/people/deleon.html

The Expedition of Narváez and Cabeza De Vaca

http://www.floridahistory.com/cabeza.html

http://www.pbs.org/weta/thewest/resources/archives/one/cabeza.htm

Hernando de Soto

http://www.floridahistory.com/inset11.html

http://www.archeologyinc.org/soto.html

Pedro Menéndez de Aviles and St. Augustine

http://www.staugustine.com/

http://www.bama.ua.edu/~prest003/pedro.htm

Index

Photo Credits

About the Authors

Bill Thompson graduated from Boston University with a degree in education. After teaching history in public schools, Mr. Thompson earned a Master of Divinity from Colgate-Rochester and became a Presbyterian minister. He pastored in New York, New Jersey, and Florida. He and his wife, Dorcas, now live in Swarthmore, Pennsylvania. Their first book, a biography of the Apache leader Geronimo, was published in 2002 by Chelsea House Publishers.

Dorcas (Boardman) Thompson graduated from Wheaton College in Illinois with a bachelor's degree in history. She taught history and social studies in Massachusetts, New York, and Pennsylvania. She has served as head librarian in a private school and worked as an editor for an educational publisher in Massachusetts. The Thompsons have one daughter, Rebecca Mandia, who is an elementary school teacher in Newtown, Pennsylvania.

HICKMANS